W9-DEJ-852

ANIMAL RIGHTS

ANIMAL RIGHTS

BY CHRISTIE R. RITTER

Content Consultant
Nathan Nobis, Ph.D.
Professor, Morehouse College

ABDO

CREDITS

Published by ABDO Publishing Company, 8000 West 78th Street, Edina, Minnesota 55439. Copyright © 2008 by Abdo Consulting Group, Inc. International copyrights reserved in all countries. No part of this book may be reproduced in any form without written permission from the publisher. The Essential Library™ is a trademark and logo of ABDO Publishing Company.

Printed in the United States.

Editor: Karen Latchana Kenney
Copy Editor: Paula Lewis
Interior Design and Production: Nicole Brecke
Cover Design: Nicole Brecke

Library of Congress Cataloging-in-Publication Data
Ritter, Christie.
 Animal rights / Christie Ritter.
     p. cm. — (Essential viewpoints)
 Includes bibliographical references and index.
 ISBN 978-1-60453-054-4
 1. Animal rights. 2. Animal welfare. 3. Animal rights—History.
I. Title.

 HV4708.R57 2008
 179'.3—dc22

                                        2007031914

TABLE OF CONTENTS

*A dog who survived cruelty walks the runway
at an ASPCA charm school show.*

THE ISSUE OF
ANIMAL RIGHTS

*M*illions of people own cats, dogs, hamsters, and even iguanas as pets. These animals are treated like family members. They receive medical attention and have plenty to eat and drink. They often die in loving arms.

Other animals have very different kinds of lives. Farm animals such as cows, chickens, and pigs are also given some veterinary care, various types of food, and fresh water. But ultimately, these animals are raised so that people can eat them. In a quest to understand and prevent human disease, scientists at laboratories experiment on millions of animals. They use mice and other animals as subjects of medical research.

Scientists who conduct experiments on animals and ranchers who raise animals for meat contend that these animals serve an important purpose: They benefit human life. But in recent years, more people have begun to consider this issue from the animals' point of view.

The Heart of the Controversy

Are animals here for the pleasure and benefit of humans? Do animals deserve any rights, such as the right to life, the right to be treated with respect, or the right to not be caused pain or suffering for others' benefit? Should they have any of the same rights as people do? Do

Americans and Their Pets

Most Americans have pets. In the United States, there are 90.5 million cats, 73.9 million dogs, 16.6 million birds, 11 million reptiles, and 18.2 million small animals such as guinea pigs and hamsters. Approximately 63 percent of U.S. homes have at least one pet.

smarter animals deserve more protection and better treatment than less intelligent species? These issues have been pondered for generations, but in recent years the controversy has become more intense.

In the 1960s, equal rights for people of all races was an important issue in the United States. Earlier in American history, women were treated as the property of their fathers or husbands. They did not have the right to vote, go to school, or do many of the things women can do today. After many years of struggle, women and all races of people gained equal rights within the U.S. legal system.

As ideas about different rights for different groups of people have changed, the debate has extended to animals. The fundamental question for some philosophers is the basic status of animals. Is it right to consider animals as human property and to harm them for human gain?

Those in favor of animal rights say that people should never use animals as a commodity or resource. They believe animals should not be used for food or scientific research. These activists argue that animals are individuals and should never be made to suffer or be denied freedom for human benefit. For these activists, it is simple—people should not use or treat animals as a commodity.

On the other side of the debate, people point out that animals have been raised for food for centuries. They believe that meat is a crucial part of the human diet and animal farming is a key component in the world economy. Also, animal rights opponents believe that finding cures and treatments for disease would not be possible without using animals in medical experiments.

"The day may come when the rest of animal creation may acquire those rights which never could have been withholden from them but by the hand of tyranny. ... The question is not, 'Can they reason? nor can they talk? but, Can they suffer?'"[1]
—*Jeremy Bentham, eighteenth-century British philosopher*

Early Animal Rights Organizations

The first organizations to prevent cruelty to animals were founded in Britain in the early nineteenth century. These groups spread across Europe and to the United States over the next century. There are now animal protection societies around the world. The American Society for the Prevention of Cruelty to Animals (ASPCA) was established in 1866. The American Humane Association (AHA) was established in 1877. And, the American Anti-Vivisection Society (AAVS) was founded in 1883. These groups are among the oldest animal protection organizations in the United States. The Animal Welfare Institute (AWI) was established in 1951 and originally focused on improving the treatment of animals used in scientific research.

Animal rights advocates are motivated by the belief that many animals, like humans, are conscious, aware, and feeling creatures. And, animals as well as humans want to avoid painful experiences. Animal rights advocates believe that we must carefully consider whether benefits for humans justify causing pain to an animal.

LAWS PROTECTING ANIMALS

There are some laws in place that govern the handling of animals. In 1966, Congress passed the Laboratory Animal Welfare

The Story of Pepper

Pepper was a dalmatian dog that disappeared from her owner's backyard in Pennsylvania in July 1965. The dog's owner saw Pepper's photograph in a newspaper along with 16 other dogs and two goats being unloaded from a dog dealer's truck. The owner's family began tracking down the dealer in an effort to get their dog back. They found that Pepper had been sold to another dog dealer in New York. The family traveled to New York to try to get her. However, they were not allowed entry to the dog dealer's property. They contacted the Animal Welfare Institute, seeking help to regain custody of their dog. Their search ended when they learned that Pepper had been sold to a New York hospital where she was used in an experiment and then euthanized.

Act. This law was passed after an incident in which a lost pet was used in a scientific experiment without its owner's consent. The law was later expanded and renamed the Animal Welfare Act (AWA). It now regulates the care and treatment of warm-blooded animals, excluding birds, rodents, and those used in farming.

In 1973, Congress passed the Endangered Species Act (ESA). This law set aside land for plants and animals threatened by extinction. Many animals had become extinct when lands were cleared for human development. According to the ESA, builders now have to ensure that developments will not harm a fragile ecosystem. The ESA makes it illegal to "harass, harm, pursue, hunt, shoot, wound, kill, trap, capture, or collect" a species listed under the act.[2] More than 1,700 threatened and endangered animals are protected under the ESA.

The Twenty-Eight Hour Law

The Twenty-Eight Hour Law of 1873 was the first law in the United States intended to prevent cruelty to animals. It states that animals must be given an opportunity to eat, drink, and rest at least once every 28 hours. The law came about because farm animals were sent to slaughterhouses on very long trips on trains. Today, trucks mainly transport animals. For years, the USDA did not believe this law applied to animals transported in trucks. In recent years, the USDA reversed its belief and now adheres to this law.

International treaties affecting animals include the United Nations Convention on International Trade in Endangered Species of Wild Fauna and Flora (CITES). The goal of CITES is to prevent international trade from endangering a species. The treaty went into effect in 1975 and has been signed by more than 150 countries.

In 1946, 15 nations joined together to form the International Whaling Commission (IWC). The group agreed on regulations such as setting limits on the number, size, and types of whales allowed to be hunted. The IWC now has 77 member countries.

Since 1986, there has been a moratorium on commercial whaling by the IWC members. This means that the member nations have halted whaling activities. However, whaling by native peoples and some scientific whaling is still allowed. It is believed that the moratorium has helped some species to increase their populations significantly.

Fishermen haul a whale aboard their ship off the coast of northern Norway.

Motorists ride past cattle in the streets of New Delhi, India, where cows are considered sacred.

ANIMALS THROUGHOUT
HISTORY

In ancient times, people often tended both crops and animals. Many people lived far from cities and had to rely on their own land to produce enough food to feed their families. Among the animals tended were sheep, goats, and cows.

People also hunted wild animals such as deer, birds, and rabbits for food. Throughout human history, fish and marine mammals have been an important resource for aboriginal, or native, peoples. This was especially true in remote areas such as Greenland, Russia, and Alaska. Whale meat was eaten and whale oil was harvested for use in heating and lighting.

CHRISTIAN AND JEWISH REFERENCES

Religious beliefs influence the way many people think about the treatment of animals. In Western cultures, where Christian and Jewish beliefs are predominant, many people use the Bible or the Torah as a guide. The theory of creation is based on Genesis, the first chapter in both of these books. There are several verses in this chapter that support the idea that animals were created for people to use.

Patron Saint of Animals

Saint Francis of Assisi is well-known as the patron saint of animals and nature. He gave up a life of wealth to help the poor, serve God, and imitate the life of Jesus by preaching nonviolence and compassion to all living things. Many Christians around the world mark the feast day of Saint Francis on October 4 in ceremonies blessing animals.

Genesis 1:28 states that humans are to,

*have dominion over the fish of the sea, and over the birds
of the air and over every living thing that moves upon the
earth.*[1]

Genesis 9:3 states, "Every moving thing that lives
shall be food for you."[2]

People who believe humans are not supposed to
eat animals point to Genesis 1:29. This verse states,

*Behold I have given you every plant yielding seed which is
upon the face of all
the earth, and every
tree with seed in its
fruit; you shall have
them for food.*[3]

Another
mention of animals
in the Bible is the
story of Noah's
Ark. Here, Noah is
asked to protect the
different species
of animals on the
earth during a great
flood.

The Dalai Lama

The Dalai Lama is the leader of Tibetan Buddhists. His followers believe that he is the latest of a long line of reincarnated spiritual leaders. The current Dalai Lama, who was born Tenzin Gyatso, is the fourteenth man to hold the title. According to the Dalai Lama,

Different forms of life at different levels of existence make up the teeming denizens of this earth of ours. And, no matter whether they belong to the higher groups such as human beings or to the lower groups such as animals, all beings primarily seek peace, comfort and security. Life is as dear to a mute creature as it is to a man. Even the lowliest insect strives for protection against dangers that threaten its life. Just as each one of us wants happiness and fears pain, just as each one of us wants to live and not to die, so do all other creatures.[4]

Hinduism

Hinduism is the predominant religion of India. Animal sacrifice is the ritual killing of animals. It is part of Hindu doctrine and has been practiced for thousands of years. But, it has become less common in modern India. Reincarnation is the concept that a person could come back in another life as some other type of creature. This idea is also a part of Hindu belief.

Sacred Cows

Cows have a special place in Indian society. The Hindu religion is practiced by the majority of Indians. According to Hinduism, cows are the most sacred of animals. They are a symbol of the divine. Cows are used in religious ceremonies and it is believed that they provide special blessings for people. In rural areas, many people own cows and rely on milk as an important part of their diet. In many parts of India, it is against the law to slaughter a cow for meat.

Buddhism

Buddhism, a religion that is popular in some parts of Asia, teaches its followers to respect all life. Buddhists also believe in the concept of reincarnation. Some sects of Buddhists, such as the Zen Buddhists, believe that people should not eat meat.

Evolution

Charles Darwin was a British scientist in the nineteenth century. His writing and research changed the way people thought about animals.

Darwin's theory of evolution
states that all living creatures
have a common ancestor. Over
millions of years, living things
have changed through adaptation
to their environment. Creatures
that adapted better survived,
reproduced, and passed on their genes. This process
is called natural selection.

"Animals, whom we have made our slaves, we do not like to consider our equal."[5]
—*Charles Darwin*

On his five-year voyage around the world,
Darwin observed that there are many similarities
between different species. Darwin was the first
to present scientific evidence that humans and
other primates, such as gorillas and chimpanzees,
had a common ancestor. His research was
groundbreaking—showing that humans and animals
are importantly similar.

Charles Darwin in 1875

Pa Pa, a ten-year-old Boston terrier, was rescued from a puppy mill.

A Philosophical Debate

The debate over the rights of animals often begins with a discussion of pain. Can animals feel pain the same way that people do? Can they feel pain like babies do? Is pain as bad, or worse, for animals, or does it not affect them?

Scientists who have studied these questions conclude that there is not one answer. People cannot know for certain if an animal feels pain. But, people can confidently believe that an animal's reaction to pain indicates that it felt the pain. For example, if a dog's tail is stepped on, the dog normally reacts by yelping.

It is more difficult to determine if animals such as insects or fish feel pain. Their brains and nervous systems are not as similar to the human brain as that of mammals. In general though, scientists agree that many animals (mammals and birds, clearly) do feel pain. Being able to sense pain is a useful tool in helping all animals learn to avoid things that cause pain, which helps them survive.

In 1892, British author Henry Salt wrote *Animal Rights*. In this book, Salt argued that animals should have the freedom to live a natural life.

Salt wrote,

> *If we must kill, whether it be man or animal, let us kill and have done with it; if we must inflict pain, let us do what is inevitable. ...*

Mammals

Humans are one of more than 5,000 species that are members of the class of mammals. Mammals are similar in that: they are warm-blooded, have hair, and the females of the species produce milk to feed their offspring. Humans are also vertebrates, meaning they have a backbone. Scientists have a better understanding of vertebrate mammals than they do of other classes of animals.

But (here is the cardinal point) let us first be assured that it is necessary.[1]

Although Salt was influential in his time, his ideas were largely forgotten until Peter Singer made many of the same points 83 years later.

Peter Singer, an Australian philosopher, wrote a book in 1975 titled *Animal Liberation*. In it, he urged people to completely change the way they thought about animals. He advocated a "principle of equality" in which pain, suffering, and other forms of ill-treatment are equally bad for whoever experiences them, regardless of their race, sex, or species. He said,

If a being suffers there can be no moral justification for refusing to take that suffering into consideration. No matter what the nature of the being, the principle of equality requires that its suffering be counted equally with the like suffering ... of any other being.[2]

ANIMALS AS EQUALS

Singer's book ignited the modern debate over animal rights. He equated the rights of animals with civil rights. He wrote,

Racists violate the principle of equality by giving greater weight to the interests of members of their own race when there is a clash between their interests and the interests of those of another race. Sexists violate the principle of equality by favoring the interests of their own sex. Similarly, speciesists allow the interests of their own species to override the greater interests of members of other species. The pattern is identical in each case.[3]

American philosopher Tom Regan believes that Singer did not go far enough in his arguments. Regan said that animals should not be viewed as human resources, but as their own individual "subjects-of-a-life."[4] Regan also states that there can be no hierarchy of value based on differences between different animals. He said,

All who have inherent value thus have it equally ... All animals are equal. One either has [value] or one does not. There are no in-betweens. Moreover, all those who have it, have it equally. It does not come in degrees.[5]

Speciesism

The term "speciesism" was coined by British psychologist Richard Ryder in 1970. It is defined as discrimination based on a certain species. Ryder argued it was similar to racism and sexism, which are other types of discrimination. Ryder states, "if we are going to care about the suffering of other humans then logically we should care about the suffering of non-humans too."[6]

Animals as Machines

The French Seventeenth-century philosopher René Descartes believed that animals were incapable of suffering. He thought that since they could not use language, they were not conscious and could not think, reason, or feel pain. He compared animals to machines. This point of view predominated for the next three centuries.

LEGAL RIGHTS OF ANIMALS

The debate over animal rights is not only philosophical but also legal. What legal rights and protections should animals have? Law professor Gary Francione says that providing for the humane treatment and welfare of animals is not the answer, since people who believe in these kinds of protections still harm animals for many purposes. He argues that "we are obligated to extend to animals only one right—the right not to be treated as the property of humans."[7] This is a radical idea, since humans have thought of animals as property for thousands of years.

Francione says animals' interests in avoiding pain and suffering and in life itself deserve equal consideration to humans' interests in the same things. This does not mean that animals and humans are the same, but instead that,

> We accept that animals have a morally significant interest in not suffering and that we must justify the necessity of inflicting any suffering on animals.[8]

The solution, he suggests, is to "stop using animals in ways in which we do not use any humans."[9]

ANIMAL INTELLIGENCE

Some people involved in the debate over animal rights suggest that intelligence is what sets humans apart from other animals. Therefore, different animals deserve different rights based on their comparative intelligence. Primates, for example, would have more and stronger rights because of their special status as the closest relatives to humans in the animal world.

But, there are many other species whose intelligence is more difficult for humans to measure. Animal

Koko

Since she was an infant, a gorilla named Koko has been the subject of a research project in animal intelligence and communication. Dr. Penny Patterson, a Stanford University-trained developmental psychologist, has taught Koko more than 1,000 American Sign Language signs. Koko has also made up some of her own signs. She uses them to communicate to humans. Koko also understands approximately 2,000 words of spoken English, some written English, and some written numbers. Koko's life and learning has been documented on film, on television, in magazine and newspaper articles, and in books.

Over the years, researchers have also learned about Koko's emotions. In 2004, Koko signed that she had a toothache. She is also famous for having her own pet animals. In 1984, she had a kitten she named All Ball, which was killed when it was run over by a car. Koko expressed her sadness by signing, "Cry, Sad, Frown."

intelligence adapts to the different environments in which a species lives. Dolphins, for example, have much better hearing than humans. They use echolocation. This is a technique of emitting sound waves and listening to the echo to find their way in the ocean. Scientists have also learned that wild dolphins have special whistle sounds that they use to communicate with each other.

"The greatness of a nation and its moral progress can be judged by the way its animals are treated. ... I hold that, the more helpless a creature, the more entitled it is to protection by man from the cruelty of man."[10]

—Mahatma Gandhi

Researchers have observed elephants using tools such as branches to dig holes. It has also been discovered that elephants communicate by using low rumbling sounds that can carry over long distances. In the wild, orangutans communicate with each other by gesturing. In captivity, they have been taught sign language by animal researchers. Other primates also have demonstrated their intelligence by using tools and sign language.

SCALE OF AUTONOMY

Law professor Steven Wise suggests rating animals on a scale of autonomy and giving them rights based on their scores. His definition of autonomy is

Koko, the famous sign language-using gorilla, celebrates her thirtieth birthday with Dr. Penny Patterson.

based on whether the animal acts intentionally and possesses a self-awareness. Humans are given a rating of 1.0 because they act intentionally and are aware of themselves. If it is unknown whether an animal acts intentionally and is self-aware, then its rating is .50. If an animal demonstrates that it is unaware of itself and there is no evidence of its acting intentionally, then its rating is less than .50.

Humans above All Else?

The theories of thirteenth-century philosopher Saint Thomas Aquinas influenced the thinking of later philosophers. He believed that animals lack reason; therefore, animals deserve no consideration by humans. He also discussed a hierarchy of creation, beginning with plants, followed by animals, then humans. Each lower form of creation served the one above it.

According to this scale, Wise has given a rating of .59 to honeybees because they use signals to communicate with each other. They also demonstrate long-term memory and the ability to learn by finding their way in a maze. Honeybees, though, do not demonstrate a sense of self. Other species on the scale include: dogs at .68, elephants at .75, parrots at .78, dolphins at .90, orangutans at .93, gorillas at .95, and bonobos (sometimes called pygmy chimpanzee) at .98. Wise suggests that animals with a rating of .90 and above should be given special rights because,

> they understand symbols, use language or a sophisticated language-like communication system, and may deceive, pretend, or imitate, and solve complex problems.[11]

These different philosophical beliefs consider the role of animals along with human society. Different groups have developed ways to ensure that animals are treated in certain ways by humans.

Attorney and author Steven Wise in his office with his cat and his dog

A PETA protest to protect birds

THE ANIMAL RIGHTS MOVEMENT

housands of animal rights groups have formed since the beginning of the movement in the 1970s. Some groups advocate for a specific animal species and others try to prevent certain practices they deem to be cruel. Other groups aim to protect the rights of farmers, hunters, and medical research facilities that use animals as subjects of their research. It is useful to take a look at some of the largest groups to understand why they were established, what they have accomplished, and where they concentrate their efforts.

In Favor: The Humane Society

The mission of the Humane Society of the United States (HSUS) is,

> to create a humane and sustainable world for all animals—a world that will also benefit people. We seek to forge a lasting and comprehensive change in human consciousness of and behavior toward all animals in order to prevent animal cruelty, exploitation, and neglect, and to protect wild habitats and the entire community of life.[1]

This organization was established in 1954. It is now one of the largest animal protection organizations in the Unites States.

In Favor: Farm Sanctuary

Against industrialized farming, Farm Sanctuary was formed to fight against the cruelties inflicted upon animals in the farming industry. It has rescued inhumanely treated animals from farms and nursed them back to health. It also seeks to educate the public about industrialized farming and advocates for animal rights laws.

In Favor: The Fund for Animals

Writer Cleveland Amory started the Fund for Animals in 1967 with the mottoes "We speak for those who can't" and "Animals have rights, too."[2] His group undertook an advertising campaign against wearing fur in 1974, featuring well-known actresses. In 1978, the group shed light on the annual Canadian hunt in which baby fur seals are clubbed

Vegetarians and Vegans

Many people who are active in the animal rights movement have chosen a vegetarian or vegan lifestyle. There are many variations on what people consider vegetarian, but the strict meaning of the word is that no meat of any animal is eaten.

Vegans eat no animal flesh and restrict all animal products from their diet. They do not eat eggs or consume any other bird, or dairy products such as milk, yogurt, and cheese, which come from cows, sheep, or goats.

Strict vegans typically eliminate animal products not only from their diet but also from their closets and homes. They do not wear or use fur, leather, wool, silk, down feathers, or skins of any kind. It was once believed that vegans and vegetarians did not get enough protein in their diets, but beans, peas, nuts, and whole grains are all excellent plant sources of protein. Being a vegan or vegetarian does not pose health risks, as long as a varied diet is eaten. In fact, medical research shows that often there are health benefits and decreased risks of high cholesterol, heart disease, obesity, some cancers, and other diseases.

to death. The following year, the group painted 1,000 seals red to make their pelts worthless to fur hunters. In 2005, the Fund for Animals joined in a partnership with the Humane Society of the United States.

IN FAVOR: PEOPLE FOR THE ETHICAL TREATMENT OF ANIMALS

People for the Ethical Treatment of Animals (PETA) was founded in 1980 and quickly became a high-profile animal rights organization. Its goal, according to cofounder Ingrid Newkirk, is to expand the compassion that people have for their companion animals, such as dogs and cats, to all animals. The group has a large membership base, which helps bring attention to its campaigns. Celebrities Pamela Anderson, Christy Turlington, Alicia Silverstone, and Kim Basinger have posed for PETA's "I'd Rather Go Naked Than Wear Fur" advertising campaign.

IN FAVOR: THE ANIMAL LIBERATION FRONT

The Animal Liberation Front (ALF) is a group that has taken a controversial approach to animal rights. In the 1970s, members raided British laboratories and freed animals used in research. Because many of the group's tactics are illegal, its members have remained anonymous. Economic sabotage, which includes destroying property and research records, is another way the group tries to accomplish its goal of ending animal suffering. Animal breeders, fur retailers, and butchers have also been targeted by the ALF. The FBI (Federal Bureau of Investigation) has designated the group as a terrorist group.

IN FAVOR: THE ANIMAL LEGAL DEFENSE FUND

The Animal Legal Defense Fund was established in 1979 to strengthen laws against animal cruelty and to enforce existing laws. This group files lawsuits and provides legal advice to prosecute animal abuse. It also serves as a resource for public education on animal law.

IN FAVOR: IN DEFENSE OF ANIMALS

In Defense of Animals (IDA) was founded by veterinarian Elliot Katz in 1983. Katz founded the group after he investigated reports of animal abuse in the laboratories of the University of California at Berkeley. The group has an international focus.

They have freed dolphins in Japan, worked to force the closure of a chimpanzee research lab in New Mexico, and organized boycotts of companies that test consumer products on animals. The group's goals include,

> *ending the exploitation and abuse of animals by raising the status of animals beyond that of mere property, and by defending their rights, welfare and habitat.*[3]

IDA has established sanctuaries for rescued animals in Mississippi and Cameroon, Africa.

HISTORIC CASES AND CAMPAIGNS OF ANIMAL RIGHTS GROUPS

Peter Singer's book, *Animal Liberation*, and his philosophy that animals deserve respect and freedom from pain was put into action by animal rights activists. Henry Spira organized the first such campaign in 1976. Spira learned that the federally funded National Institutes of Health had granted money for the

Foie Gras

Foie gras is the name of the fatty liver of a goose, which some consider a gourmet delicacy. PETA and other animal rights groups have worked to outlaw the sale of foie gras, based on the way it is produced. Male geese are fed up to four pounds (1.8 kg) of grain two or three times a day using a tube placed in their throats. The animals' livers swell up to ten times their normal size as a result. California voters approved a ban on the sale of foie gras in 2004. The law will go into effect in 2012. The city of Chicago banned foie gras in 2006. It is also illegal in many countries, including Ireland, Denmark, Switzerland, Germany, and Italy.

American Museum of Natural History in Manhattan to do research on cats. The experiments involved removing parts of the animals' brains and destroying some of their nerves and senses. Protests began at the museum. They were followed by a letter-writing campaign, bomb threats, and intense media coverage. In less than two years, the cat laboratory was shut down.

THE DRAIZE TEST

After the success of his first campaign, Spira turned his focus to cosmetic testing on animals. Products such as shampoo and eye makeup were being tested on the eyes of white rabbits in a procedure called the Draize test. No anesthesia was used and some rabbits were blinded by the products being tested. Spira wanted to convince Revlon, one of the largest cosmetics companies, to find alternatives to animal testing. Through letter-writing campaigns to the company, boycotts of stores that sold the products, and coverage of the issue by the media, the company felt pressured to change its practices. Revlon donated $750,000 to scientific research aimed at finding an alternative to the Draize test. Soon thereafter, Avon matched the donation.

Many cosmetics companies have since implemented policies banning or restricting animal testing.

Exposing a Laboratory

Alex Pacheco, cofounder of PETA, volunteered to work at a neurological research laboratory in Silver Spring, Maryland, in 1981. He photographed and kept a journal about the treatment the monkeys received and the dirty, small cages in which they were housed. He then brought five veterinarians and primatologists to the lab to see the conditions. Together, they convinced local police that anticruelty laws were being violated. Police searched the lab and removed the monkeys. The publicity from the episode resulted in a public outcry. This galvanized the animal rights movement and helped make PETA the largest animal rights group in the United States.

Save the Whales

Groups often work together on behalf of a certain species under threat. The campaign to "Save the

Jane Goodall and the Chimps

For more than 40 years, Jane Goodall has studied chimpanzees in Tanzania, Africa. Her research in the field of primatology has provided great insight into the private lives and societies of the species.

Today, Goodall's research continues and is currently the longest-running study of an animal species in its natural environment. The Jane Goodall Institute, which she founded in 1977, works to protect chimpanzees and their habitats.

Whales" was a concerted effort by organizations both inside and outside the animal rights movement. They focused their attention on the dwindling whale population. Some of the groups involved included the Fund for Animals, Greenpeace, the Animal Welfare Institute, and the Sea Shepherd Conservation Society. In 1986, a moratorium was declared on commercial whaling.

HUNTING SEALS

The effort to stop the annual hunt of seals in Canada began in the 1960s and still continues. Those who oppose the hunting of seals voice their opinions through boycotts of Canadian seafood and informational campaigns. As a result, some countries have banned the import of seal fur, and Canada has placed quotas on the number of seals that hunters can take.

FUR-FREE FRIDAY

Since 1986, Fur-Free Friday has been held on the day after Thanksgiving. Animal rights activists in cities around the United States stage demonstrations outside department stores that sell fur. Activists do this to draw attention to what they consider to be the

Members of the HSUS protest against fur on a Fur-Free Friday.

cruel practices of the fur industry. Demonstrators
have picketed with signs showing pictures of animals
being skinned, shouted at people wearing fur, and
smashed windows of stores selling fur. While sales
of fur were down in the late 1980s and early 1990s,
sales increased beginning in the mid-1990s and have
remained steady.

PROCTER & GAMBLE

In 1989, In Defense of Animals began a boycott of consumer goods manufacturer Procter & Gamble to protest the company's animal testing. Procter & Gamble tested its products, such as shampoo, toothpaste, and laundry detergent, in its laboratories. In Defense of Animals claimed that the tests were outdated, not required by law, and the company was involved with "blinding, burning, maiming and killing" thousands of animals each year.[4] In 2005, the company formed a partnership with the Humane Society of the United States to develop alternatives to testing consumer products on animals.

OPPOSED: THE RIGHT TO USE ANIMALS FOR SPORT AND MEDICAL RESEARCH

Some groups believe that the right to hunt animals and use them for medical research is something that should be protected and defended.

The U.S. Sportsmen's Alliance was formed to defeat a 1977 Ohio ballot measure that would have banned trapping in that state. The group united hunters, fishermen, and trappers to defend their right to trap animals, which they consider part of their American heritage. The ballot measure was defeated. The group continues to lobby for public and government support of hunting, trapping, fishing, and wildlife management.

The National Animal Interest Alliance was created in 1991 and is composed of animal breeders, research scientists, farmers, hunters, and veterinarians, a varied group that supports "responsible animal ownership and use."[5] They believe that many medical advances have been made as a result of animal testing. They also believe that hunting and fishing provide opportunities for family recreation and serve as wildlife management tools.

Americans for Medical Progress is a group composed of people who work in the field of medical research and people who have benefited from medical research. The group works to nurture "public understanding of

Environmental Allies

Those concerned with the environment often have overlapping interests with those concerned with animals, especially wildlife. The Sierra Club, the Nature Conservancy, Greenpeace, the National Resources Defense Council, and the Earth Island Institute are a few organizations that promote the protection of the earth's delicate ecosystem.

and support for the humane, necessary and valuable use of animals in medicine."[6] They believe that all people receive the benefits of animal research through the use of medicines we have today.

Opposed: Animal Enterprise Terrorism Act

Businesses opposed to the tactics of animal rights advocates have urged lawmakers to punish protesters who advocate violence or damage property. In 2006, Congress approved the Animal Enterprise Terrorism Act. It increases federal penalties on people convicted of interfering with, threatening, or harming people or businesses involved with animals. Opponents of the act say it will limit free speech and is so vague that any business could claim that it is a victim of "terrorism." ⏤

A hunter displays his trophy deer.

Sows in restrictive pens on a farm near Janesville, Iowa

ANIMALS AS FOOD AND CLOTHING

The most common way that people use animals is for food. In the United States, more than 8 billion chickens, 252 million turkeys, 104 million pigs, and 34 million cattle are slaughtered annually for food. In addition, millions of sheep and ducks, as well as more than a billion farmed fish are processed for food each year in this country. Many American farms have changed from small family enterprises to intensive and efficiency-driven corporations. These kinds of farms can handle the large-scale food production that is demanded in the United States today to produce inexpensive meat, eggs, and dairy products.

Because of the economic pressures to produce meat at low prices, farms have become similar to factories. Animal rights groups have focused much of their energy in recent years at this new industry of "factory farming." This term was coined in 1964, by British writer Ruth Harrison, in *Animal Machines*. She wrote,

> *Life in the factory farm revolves entirely around profits, and animals are accessed purely for their ability to convert food into flesh or "saleable products."*[1]

Factory farming is also known as "industrialized farming."

"Now more than ever, America is a Nation of meat eaters. In 2000, total meat consumption (red meat, poultry, and fish) reached 195 pounds ... per person, fifty-seven pounds above average annual consumption in the 1950s. Each American consumed an average of seven pounds more red meat than in the 1950s, forty-six pounds more poultry, and four pounds more fish and shellfish."[2]
—USDA Agriculture Fact Book 2001–2002

A Slaughtering Law

In 1978, Congress passed the Humane Methods of Slaughter Act (HMSA). This act states that when humane methods of slaughtering are used, livestock do not needlessly suffer. Rules were put in place to follow one of two methods that are deemed humane.

The first method, which applies specifically to cattle, calves, horses, mules, sheep, and pigs, requires that animals be,

> rendered insensible to pain by a single blow or gunshot or an electrical, chemical or other means that is rapid and effective, before being shackled, hoisted, thrown, cast, or cut.[3]

A second method, in which the animal's throat is cut without first being stunned, is allowed for religious purposes.

The National Animal Interest Alliance

Industries that support industrialized farming, such as the National Animal Interest Alliance, say,

> Modern American agricultural methods supply us with an unprecedented bounty of quality meat, eggs and dairy products and with leather, wool, furs, and myriad items derived from animal byproducts. The vast majority of Americans enjoy these products as part of a well-balanced diet or lifestyle.[4]

They also say the practice of using animals for food is a proud tradition:

> *Livestock farming represents an ancient partnership between animals and man. Sheep, cattle, goats, and poultry have sustained human families for millennia and have made civilization possible.*[5]

POULTRY

Livestock farms must abide by the HMSA. However, the HMSA law does not apply to poultry, which constitutes the vast majority of animals slaughtered. More than 1 million chickens are killed every hour in the United States. Many animal rights groups are encouraging the government to broaden the HMSA to include poultry.

Chickens are usually hung upside down and stunned in an electrified water bath. Then their throats are slit and they are dipped into hot defeathering tanks. Some chicken ranches are using a new slaughtering technique called Controlled

"It is my view that the vegetarian manner of living by its purely physical effect on the human temperament would most beneficially influence the lot of mankind."[6]

—*Albert Einstein*

Atmosphere Killing (CAK). This method allows animals to remain in their shipping crates at the slaughterhouse. The crates are then sent through a chamber containing an inert gas that makes the birds unconscious. They die from anoxia, a lack of oxygen, but the meat is not affected.

The National Chicken Council states that,

Domestic animals are adaptable to a variety of conditions. Today's chicken has been purposefully selected to thrive under modern management. We believe current good management practices that avoid destructive behavior, prevent disease, and promote good health and production, are consistent with the generally accepted criteria of humane treatment. [7]

Because factory farms are large-scale operations, there can be tens of thousands of fowl housed together under one roof. Flocks live together in tightly confined areas and disease can spread quickly. This has resulted in the use of more antibiotics and other medicines in the poultry. Critics say these practices pose a risk to human health because viruses can become resistant to drugs. And, humans may have unknown side effects from eating chickens given the antibiotics.

Egg Production

The average American consumes 250 eggs each year. There are approximately 300 million laying hens in the United States. Modern hens have been bred for increased egg production and each one produces an average of 250 eggs annually. This is far greater than their wild ancestors. To produce billions of eggs, modern factory farming techniques have been introduced.

The modern practice of confining laying hens in battery cages has drawn sharp criticism in recent years. Battery cages are made of wire and stacked in rows inside warehouses. As many as 250,000 hens are housed in a single building. Each cage measures approximately 18 by 20 inches (46 by 51 cm). Three to eight birds live in each cage. The floors of the cages slope so that the eggs roll forward and can be gathered automatically.

Designing a Better Death

Animal scientist Temple Grandin has developed new livestock handling practices and designed facilities for slaughterhouses in an effort to reduce an animal's fear and pain. "Treating animals in a humane manner is the right thing to do,"[8] Grandin says. Grandin's animal research has led her to believe that all animals, including rats, birds, and reptiles, suffer from pain.

According to the American Egg Board,

Most new construction favors the cage system because of its sanitation and efficiency. ... Because care and feeding of hens, maintenance, sanitation and egg gathering all take time and money, there is a strong trend toward automation whenever possible.[9]

The use of battery cages has been criticized because the hens cannot perform natural behaviors in the cages, such as spreading their wings, walking, or building a nest. Also, the wire floors can cause injuries to the hens' feet or lead to deformities in their claws. As a result, they exhibit stressful behaviors, such as plucking their feathers or pecking each other. It is standard practice to remove the beaks of the chickens to prevent them from injuring each other.

In Europe, campaigns have been fought to outlaw the use of battery cages in egg production. They are being phased out in the countries of the European Union and will be banned by 2012. Consumers in many countries refuse to buy eggs produced using battery cages and some supermarkets have stopped selling them. Campaigns are underway in the United States to phase out battery cages.

A chicken farm near Lake Stevens, Washington

Male chicks are a byproduct of the egg production process. Since they do not lay eggs and their gender is not the preferred type for meat, they are disposed of shortly after hatching. They are killed by poisonous gas, ground up alive, or thrown into dumpsters to suffocate or die of dehydration. More than 200 million chicks produced by the egg industry meet this fate each year.

Dairy Industry

More than 8 million milk cows in the United States produce approximately 20 billion gallons (75 billion L) of milk annually. Each cow produces approximately seven gallons (27 L) of milk each day. Dairy cows, like all mammals, produce milk to feed their offspring. In order to keep producing milk, they must give birth once a year. Their offspring are taken away so that the milk they produce is not consumed by the calves, but can be collected for human consumption. The female offspring of dairy calves become part of the dairy herd and the males are used for meat.

The average size of a dairy herd has increased from six cows in 1950 to 25 in 1975. By 2003, the average had increased to 106. Animal rights critics have raised concerns over the increasing herd size, which parallels the industrialization of farming in general.

Consumers Push for Change

As concern for animal welfare has grown among consumers, some retailers and producers have created special labels for cruelty-free products. One such organization is the Animal Compassion

Foundation, established by Whole Foods Market.

The organization recognizes that modern agriculture is at a turning point. According to the Animal Compassion Foundation's Web site,

> *The quest for cheap food has created an industrialized model of meat production in which animals are bred and raised in conditions focused on efficiency rather than the basic needs of the animals. The abilities and skills necessary to raise farm animals with their welfare and well-being as the top priority have become lost in this model.*[10]

Whole Foods began developing standards in 2003 that producers are required to meet in order for their products to be labeled "Animal Compassionate." The AWI has also developed the "Animal Welfare Approved" seal, which can only be earned by independent family farms.

Retailers have found that informed consumers want a choice.

Veal

Veal is the name given to the meat of the male offspring of a dairy cow. The production of veal involves removing the calf from its mother almost immediately after it is born and confining it in a very small crate. The confinement prevents the animal's muscles from developing. Lack of muscle and a low-iron, milk-based diet produces a pale, white meat. Calves are slaughtered at approximately 18 weeks of age. The popularity of veal is in decline in the United States. In 2004, voters in Arizona approved a proposition banning the small crates in which veal calves are confined. In August 2007, the American Veal Association proposed phasing out the crates over a ten-year period.

They may be willing to pay extra for eggs produced by hens not kept in battery cages.

Restaurants are also responding to animal welfare concerns. Burger King announced its intention to buy a percentage of its eggs from cage-free producers. It also has said it will buy its chicken from producers that use the more humane CAK slaughter method.

In 1997, McDonald's hired Dr. Temple Grandin, an expert on animal behavior and designer of humane livestock handling facilities, to help the company set up a program to inspect its suppliers. The goal was to ensure that animals raised for meat for McDonald's were treated humanely before being slaughtered. McDonald's has also said it favors the development of the CAK slaughter method for poultry and would support alternatives to gestation crates for pigs.

HUNTING

Most Americans eat meat, but few are actively involved in killing the animals they eat. Humans have hunted for thousands of years. In the United States today, there are few subsistence hunters (those who need to hunt to feed themselves or their families).

Most hunters now hunt for sport. In the 1950s, approximately 10 percent of Americans hunted. In 2000, it had decreased to 6 percent. Those who hunt defend it as part of their traditional way of life.

Hunters are required to buy licenses that are issued by state-run wildlife departments. The money raised by selling licenses goes to conservation and wildlife management. Other regulations govern hunting, such as designating certain times of the year when hunting is prohibited in protected areas, the type of weapons allowed, and the limits on the number of animals that can be taken.

Pigs and People

On most factory farms, pregnant female pigs live in gestation crates. This is a metal cage with a concrete floor. They spend approximately four months confined in this space, which is barely bigger than they are.

Animal rights advocates have waged campaigns to end the practice of using gestation crates for pigs. Voters in Arizona and Florida approved a ban on the crates. The European Union has also passed a ban, which will phase out the crates by 2013.

North Carolina, Iowa, and Minnesota have more pigs than people. Large-scale pig farming has raised concern not only among animal rights advocates but also among environmentalists. Giant pig farms produce pollution, which runs into streams, rivers, lakes, bays, and oceans. In 1995, waste from a pig farm leaked into a North Carolina river and killed 10,000 fish.

Factory farms affect human health, too. A survey of drinking water wells in North Carolina found that 10 percent of the wells had unsafe levels of nitrates, a pollutant that can be traced to pig manure from nearby factory farms.

Ryland Loos, who is a hunter advocate from New York, says,

> *People who hunt have most often been the ones who come to love and appreciate these animals enough to make their welfare a life's dedication. Spending contemplative hours and days with wildlife heightens rather than diminishes the hunter's reverence for life.*[11]

Hunters believe they are providing a service by thinning populations that could cause issues if the populations grew too large. Deer, for example, are a hazard to drivers in rural areas. Hunters help keep roads safer, they contend, by reducing deer numbers. They also cite that deer overpopulation may cause many deer to starve during the winter due to lack of an abundance of food.

Canned hunts are an area of concern for animal rights groups. A canned hunt is a private ranch where sport hunters pay a price to shoot animals. Hunters can choose which type of animal they want to kill and pay according to the rarity of the species. Some of these ranches, also called "shooting preserves" or "game ranches," stock exotic African animals that have been purchased from middlemen who bought them from zoos or circuses.

A red fox caught in a trap

Trapping and Fur

Animal trapping is usually done for the animal's fur. This fur is used to make coats, hats, and other apparel. According to the Fur Free Alliance, it takes 15 to 20 foxes, 60 to 80 minks, or 27 to 30 raccoons to make a fur coat.

Animal rights advocates consider trapping to be one of the most cruel and inhumane abuses of animals because the use of animals for fur is based on fashion. Traps can also catch pets that may linger for days before dying of thirst, blood loss, or being eaten by predators.

Steel-jawed traps catch an animal by a leg and tighten as the animal tries to escape. Often, the animal chews off its own limb in an attempt to escape. These traps have been outlawed in eight states and 89 countries but are still the most commonly used traps in the United States. The United States is the world's largest provider of wild-caught fur.

According to animal rights advocates, the concept of wearing fur is morally wrong. They have organized campaigns against wearing fur and to ban the steel-jaw traps. Animal rights advocates also oppose leather, which is the treated skin of cows and pigs, and sheep's wool. Both, they say, lead to unnecessary pain, suffering, and the death of animals. ⌐

Activists of People for Animals at the Delhi International leather fair

Laboratory rats in cages

ANIMAL USE IN
SCIENTIFIC RESEARCH

Using animals to help improve human
health is an issue that divides many
animal advocates. Is it right to use animals in medical
testing? Surveys indicate that most Americans agree
that it is, but this issue has stirred controversy.

BIOMEDICAL RESEARCH

In 1628, British doctor William Harvey used animals in medical experiments to discover how blood circulates. He published his findings in his book, *On the Movement of the Heart and Blood in Animals.* His research, which involved removing the beating hearts of living animals, is considered to be one of the most important contributions in the history of medicine. The practice of cutting open a living animal for scientific research is called vivisection. By the eighteenth century, there was widespread protest in Britain against vivisection. In 1894, a vaccine against the deadly disease diphtheria was developed using animals, and antivivisectionists lost influence on public opinion.

Using animals in research does not necessarily mean using surgical procedures. Many tests are done on the skin and eyes of an animal. Approximately 20 million animals are subjects of scientific research in the United States. Most of the animals used are bred specifically for that purpose. The research is done by pharmaceutical companies, universities, hospitals, and the government.

Each project must include a committee to oversee its work with animals. The committee is called an

Pound Seizure

Pound seizure is the term used for the release of animals held at public or private shelters or agencies (sometimes called "the pound") to facilities that use them in scientific research or education. In order to give owners a chance to reclaim their pets, there is a waiting period before the animals can be euthanized or turned over for research.

Institutional Animal Care and Use Committee. It requires researchers to justify their need for animals, select the most appropriate species for the purpose of their study, and use the fewest number of animals possible.

The AWA governs the use of animals in research, although it excludes rodents. Approximately 95 percent of all animals used in scientific laboratories are mice and rats. The genetic makeup of these animals is approximately 85 percent the same as that of people. Scientists believe that testing a substance on a rodent is likely to produce similar results as it would on a human. The American Medical Association (AMA) supports the use of animals for medical education and research and opposes including rodents under the AWA protection.

Animal rights advocates say animals cannot give their consent to be used in experiments, so it is unethical to do so. They believe there are many alternatives to using animals in tests, such as computer models, human cell and tissue cultures, and clinical trials using humans. Furthermore, there are many people who do not have basic health care or access to a doctor and existing medical technology. One alternative would be to better ensure that they get this rather than experiment on animals.

Researchers counter that they do not make the decision to use an animal in research until they have studied the feasibility of alternatives. Scientists follow a policy called the "Three Rs." First, tests have been refined so they are done as humanely as possible. Second, the number of animals being used in studies has been reduced. Third, replacements are found for using animals whenever possible.

Many scientists defend the practice of continued use of animals in research. According to the Foundation for Biomedical Research,

> Nearly every major medical advance of the twentieth century has depended largely on research with animals. Our best hope for developing preventions, treatments and cures for diseases such as Alzheimer's, AIDS, and cancer will also involve biomedical research using animals.[1]

Some extreme animal rights groups have tried to halt research by vandalizing laboratories, attacking scientists, and threatening companies that use animals in research with violence. In response, the U.S. government passed regulations including the 2006 Animal Enterprise Terrorism Act, which makes it a crime to harass companies involved in animal research and their affiliates. The law also imposes fines on activists convicted of these crimes.

Vaccines

Dozens of vaccines have been developed to save humans from contracting diseases such as tetanus, polio, measles, and chicken pox. Many of these vaccines were developed using animals in research. Researchers test how an animal's immune system reacts to the introduction of a vaccine in its body. Scientists spend years testing vaccines on animals before humans receive a newly developed vaccine.

Vaccines have also been developed for animals, including one which prevents the spread of disease such as cowpox among herds of livestock. Vaccines can protect pets from contracting deadly diseases such as rabies, which can also affect people.

Chimpanzees and Other Great Apes

Because of their similarity to humans, chimpanzees were once a favorite subject of medical researchers. At one time, 90,000 chimpanzees were used annually in experiments. Originally, infant chimpanzees were caught in the wild in Africa and imported to the United States and other countries for medical research.

In 1977, chimpanzees were placed on the United Nations CITES list of Endangered Species. Since the passage of CITES in 1975, chimpanzees used for medical research in the United States have come primarily from captive breeding programs. The use of chimpanzees in biomedical research has been banned in Britain, New Zealand, Sweden, and the Netherlands. The use of chimpanzees in biomedical research is still legal in the United States.

Public concern over research on chimps led to the passage of the Chimpanzee Health Improvement and Maintenance Protection Act (CHIMP Act) in 2000. This law

"I had bought two male chimps from a primate colony in Holland. They lived next to each other in separate cages for several months before I used one as a (heart) donor. When we put him to sleep in his cage in preparation for the operation, he chattered and cried incessantly. We attached no significance to this, but it must have made a great impression on his companion, for when we removed the body to the operating room, the other chimp wept bitterly and was inconsolable for days. The incident made a deep impression on me. I vowed never again to experiment with such sensitive creatures."[2]
—*Christiaan Barnard, surgeon who performed the first human heart transplant*

provides federal support to retire chimpanzees not active or needed in research and also allows them to be brought back into research if needed. The CHIMP Act prohibits breeding and euthanasia under most circumstances.

Some researchers say that using chimps in research is unethical and a waste of money. The genetic differences between humans and chimps are important and studies on Human Immunodeficiency Virus (HIV) and Acquired Immune Deficiency Syndrome (AIDS), have proven that. In the search for a cure for HIV and AIDS, chimps have been infected with the virus but have not developed the disease, confounding researchers. According to British medical

Animals in Space

The first astronauts were animals, not people. Scientists were not sure what effect the force of takeoff would have on the human body, and the long-term effects of weightlessness were also unknown. As early as 1946, the National Aeronautics and Space Administration (NASA) began animal tests by launching fruit flies and monkeys on rockets. The Soviet Union sent former stray dog Laika aboard *Sputnik 2* in 1957, and she became the first living creature to orbit the earth. Laika is believed to have survived for ten days, but the *Sputnik 2* burned up in the atmosphere. The United States sent trained chimpanzees into space as part of the preparation for manned space flight. A four-year-old chimp named Ham flew on January 31, 1961, and survived the *Mercury* spacecraft's landing. He was trained to perform simple tasks, such as pulling levers for space flight. Ham became a celebrity after his successful flight.

scientist Jarrod Bailey, ending research on chimps and other primates:

> would benefit human medicine by halting the flow of unreliable data from it, and by diverting research funds to more appropriate and promising methods.[3]

The Great Ape Project seeks to end the exploitation of humans' nearest relatives: chimpanzees, bonobos, gorillas, and orangutans. The authors of a "Declaration on Great Apes" have asked the United Nations to recognize that these species deserve basic rights. These rights include the right to life, the protection of individual liberty, and the prohibition of torture.

DISSECTION AND ANIMALS IN MEDICAL EDUCATION

It used to be common practice for medical students to spend time in a live animal laboratory. Future doctors would practice surgical techniques or inject drugs into an anesthetized animal, often a dog. In 1985, an animal laboratory class was a part of the training at all medical schools in the United States. Now, 85 percent of U.S. medical schools have stopped the practice. The use of

"I believe I am not interested to know whether vivisection produces results that are profitable to the human race or doesn't. ...The pains which it inflicts upon unconsenting animals is the basis of my enmity toward it, and it is to me sufficient justification of the enmity without looking further."[4]

—Mark Twain,
May 26, 1899

animals in medical education has been steadily declining since 1994. Replacements include the observation of human surgery, using mannequins with removable parts, using computer software programs, and watching videos documenting vivisections and dissections of different animals.

Dissection is the process of cutting up the tissue of a plant or animal to learn about its structure. Dissection has been a part of science classes for many years. The most commonly used animal for dissection is the frog. Earthworms, fetal pigs, rats, mice, cats, and fish are also used. Animal rights groups say that using animals in science education should be done in a way that instills respect for all living things. They believe dissecting animals may have the opposite effect.

There have always been students who have found the prospect of dissecting an animal disgusting and inhumane. In some cases, these students were urged away from the field of science as a result. Now, there are policies in 14 states that require students in grades kindergarten through 12 to opt in if they choose to participate in dissection. Where no statewide policy exists, some school districts have implemented a similar opt-in policy. Parents are notified that an animal will be used for science education purposes. Parents can discuss the lesson plan with their children. Together they can choose whether to participate or use an alternative, such as computer software that offers virtual dissection or a model of the animal.

COSMETIC TESTING

Federal laws require that all new medical devices, procedures, and drugs be tested on animals before they are used on humans. There is no law requiring manufacturers of household products such as shampoo, toothpaste, or detergent to test those items on animals. Yet, many do so. Common tests involve placing a product in a rabbit's eyes, which can be done at doses that blind the animal. Many skin tests are also done which can cause severe burns to the test subjects.

Animal rights groups are concerned about these tests, which they consider unnecessary and inhumane. Animal advocates in Europe successfully lobbied for a ban on the use of animals in cosmetic testing beginning in 2009. A ban on sales of all cosmetic products tested on animals throughout the member countries of the European Union goes into effect in 2013. Some manufacturers have begun using the label "cruelty free" on their products to indicate that animals either were not used in testing or were treated humanely. Because the label does not carry any legal requirements, some critics have said it is meaningless.

In the United States, a coalition of animal rights interest groups has formed the Coalition for Consumer Information on Cosmetics (CCIC). This coalition creates a comprehensive standard for acceptable products. Its internationally recognized leaping bunny logo on products indicates that the ingredients in the cosmetic and household products have not been tested on animals. PETA has its own bunny logo and "Caring Consumer" Web site. ⌐

*Ham the Chimp was the first higher primate
to be launched into outer space on January 31, 1961.*

A pet cockatiel in its cage

ANIMALS AS PETS

sk most people if they like animals
and they will talk about their pets.
Cats, dogs, rabbits, guinea pigs, even goldfish are
considered family members by many people. That
alone is a problem for some animal advocates. Why

do people think of dogs as members of the family, while considering chickens nothing more than a choice on the menu? For some in the animal rights community, the term "pet" is considered to be something of an insult to animals. The term "companion animal" is often used as a replacement for "pet," as it is considered more respectful among animal rights activists.

IDA has led a campaign to change the wording of official documents from pet owner to "animal guardian." The group believes that doing so can help people take the role of protecting the animals in their care more seriously.

Not everyone agrees with the idea of guardianship. The National Animal Interest Alliance (NAIA) opposes the idea because they do not believe animals should be given legal rights.

OVERPOPULATION AND RESCUE ORGANIZATIONS

Organizations such as the ASPCA, local humane societies, and animal rescue groups, serve as resources for people to find pets and to offer advice on their care. These groups encourage people to adopt animals from shelters or rescue groups rather than buy them from pet stores or breeders. They also set up spay and neuter programs to tackle the pet overpopulation problem. It is estimated that approximately 5 million animals are euthanized each year in the United States because homes cannot be found for lost or unwanted pets that end up at shelters or animal control agencies.

Animal Rescuers

Most cities have an animal control agency that is in charge of rescuing injured animals, rounding up and providing temporary shelter for stray animals, and enforcing licensing requirements. Some also provide animal care information to pet owners including spay and neutering service or referral. These are publicly funded government agencies. Private organizations such as humane societies and breed-specific rescue organizations also provide temporary shelter, usually to animals that have been voluntarily given up by their owners.

Puppy mills are businesses that mass-produce purebred dogs for retail sale. Puppies born at puppy mills tend to be treated poorly and live in crowded and dirty conditions. They often endure long journeys to get to their buyers. Because of the stressful conditions and the likelihood of inbreeding, these dogs are often unhealthy.

Animal advocates agree that euthanasia is the best option for some animals. There are "no-kill shelters," which have pledged not to put any animals to death unless they are deemed unfit for adoption. But, there are many more that do not have this policy because they simply do not have

*Betty Martin, president of LIFE House for Animals,
a no-kill shelter in Frankfort, Kentucky*

the money, space, or staff to care for the unwanted
animals that come to them. For those that must
be euthanized, the HSUS, AHA, PETA, and most
other groups agree that the most humane method is
by intravenous injection of sodium pentobarbital.
This causes the animal to become unconscious and
then stop breathing before his or her heart stops
beating. This is also the method that veterinarians
recommend when a pet is suffering from illness or
injury with no chance of recovery.

Cosmetic Surgery

Animal rights groups tend not to be directly involved in pet adoptions but rather in addressing issues about pet ownership. Among these issues are the practices of declawing cats, debarking dogs, and cropping the ears or tails of certain breeds of dogs. Animal rights groups believe these surgeries can cause pain to the animals and are unnecessary and unnatural.

Some veterinarians now refuse to perform the declawing surgery on cats, which removes the last joint of the animal's toes. Vets opposed to the procedure and many animal advocates consider it a form of mutilation. Declawing a cat is illegal in some countries, including Britain and Japan. Local ordinances prevent the procedure in some U.S. cities.

The Pet Protection Act

The U.S. Congress passed the Pet Protection Act in 1990, an amendment to the Animal Welfare Act (AWA). The amendment imposes a five-day holding period before animal dealers, exhibitors, or agencies can dispose of or sell dogs and cats to research facilities. The goal of the law is to give owners a chance to find their pet if it is lost.

Docking, Cropping, and Debarking

Dogs express themselves with their tails. They wag them when they are happy and communicate fear by hiding them between their legs. But some breeds of dogs traditionally have had their tails cut short, or "docked." This is usually done when the puppy is only a few days old and without the use of anesthesia or pain relief. Some breeders say the reason for continuing to dock the tails of some types of spaniels, Dobermans, and rottweilers is so that they can compete in competitions that showcase purebred dogs. Others claim that tail docking helps prevent accidents in dogs used for hunting and herding.

Ear cropping is another cosmetic procedure that is routinely performed on some breeds of purebred puppies, particularly boxers, Great Danes, and some terriers. The puppy is usually eight to ten weeks old when it undergoes the surgery to shorten its naturally floppy ears. After surgery, the ears are taped in order to make them stand up, which is the traditional look for show dogs of these breeds. The American Veterinary Medical Association (AVMA) states that tail docking and ear cropping can cause pain and distress and should not be done for cosmetic reasons. Animal rights groups have petitioned breed clubs and dog shows to stop encouraging ear cropping and tail docking.

Debarking is a procedure that surgically alters a dog's vocal chords. It has been ordered by cities upon owners of dogs that bark excessively and disturb neighbors. The AVMA approves of the procedure only as a final alternative if all other attempts to change the dog's behavior have failed.

WILD PETS, BIRDS, AND FISH

Cats and dogs are not the only pets in American homes, of course. Animals such as birds, fish, and reptiles are also popular choices as pets. The main concern for animal rights advocates with these choices is that some of the exotic animals are captured in the wild, which upsets the balance of natural ecosystems. Wild animals also do not make the best pets.

Mutts and Champions

Most veterinarians agree that the healthiest dogs are mixed breeds or "mutts." Purebreds are much more prone to certain health issues, such as hip dysplasia in German shepherds, ear infections in cocker spaniels, and respiratory problems in bulldogs. All of these health issues are attributable to selective breeding.

According to American Kennel Club guidelines, dogs must meet certain requirements to compete in dog shows for their breed. These are very exacting guidelines and any variance from the ideal could result in disqualification from competition. Because of the popularity of these competitions and the high value placed on winners of dog shows for breeding purposes, breeders select certain characteristics when choosing mates for a dog. These characteristics, such as a very pushed-in appearance to the nose on bulldogs, can lead to health problems such as a difficulty in breathing. Animal rights advocates criticize the practice of selective breeding, saying animal health suffers because of the human desire to have a "champion" dog.

According to animal rights advocates, birds are not meant to be confined to a cage, especially alone. Birds live in flocks, often mating for life, and are very intelligent creatures with a sophisticated communication system. Confining a bird to a cage is considered inhumane. Birds often rebel against captivity, screaming or plucking out their feathers. Another issue is that some birds can live to be 100 years old, so bird care is a long-term commitment.

Tropical fish are often taken from fragile coral reefs. This can disrupt these unique and endangered ecosystems. Divers who capture these colorful fish often use techniques that can harm both the reef and the fish. Goldfish, which come from fish farms, are often kept in tiny bowls without proper filters, where they may suffocate due to lack of oxygen in their water.

Reptiles are a particular problem as pets because they often carry salmonella, a disease easily passed on to humans who touch them. The HSUS recommends against reptiles as pets since most are caught in the wild. Most people are not equipped to properly care for a reptile, which has special dietary and habitat needs. An iguana, for example, can grow to be five feet (1.5 m) long. This can be a problem for owners

Doris Day

Doris Day was one of Hollywood's most popular actresses from the 1950s to the 1980s. She made a second career in the field of animal welfare. The group she founded in 1987, The Doris Day Animal League, has worked on many pet-related issues. The focus has been on passing laws designed to help protect animals from abuse. The group merged with the HSUS in 2006.

trying to find an enclosure big enough to handle an adult iguana, not to mention a steady food supply and the required amount of ultraviolet light that many reptiles require to be healthy. ⌐

*Tim Curran, certified reptile specialist and owner of a reptile shop,
holds a rhino iguana.*

*Two performers pose with a Bengal tiger
at the Ringling Brothers and Barnum & Bailey Circus.*

ANIMAL USE IN EDUCATION
AND ENTERTAINMENT

or most people, zoos are the only place
where they can see some of the most rare
and majestic creatures found in nature. Lions,
pandas, tigers, hippos, and rhinos in their native
environment are a very long and expensive airplane

ride away. The chance to see these animals at a zoo has led to the widespread appreciation of these species. Nevertheless, animal rights advocates hope to see an end to the captivity of wild animals. They argue that zoos, marine parks, and aquariums are an outdated idea that subjects individual animals to a lifetime of miserable confinement. Animal rights advocates also believe that highly intelligent animals such as primates, dolphins, and elephants suffer greatly in captivity. Many are killed or die in the process of being captured and transported to zoos.

Some believe that zoos and aquariums provide an essential role in educating the public about the world of nature, which they could not otherwise see in person. In addition, zoos help conserve species that are endangered in their native habitats. California condors, Arabian oryx, and Przewalski's horses have all been reintroduced into their wild habitat after breeding programs at zoos increased their populations from the verge of extinction.

Freeing Keiko

Keiko was the orca, or killer whale, who starred in the 1993 film *Free Willy*, a story of a boy who helped free a captive orca. Fans of the movie led an effort to free Keiko, who languished in an aquarium in Mexico City. With help from many animal welfare organizations, Keiko was moved from Mexico and rehabilitated at the Oregon Coast Aquarium for several years. In 1998, he was released into the ocean off Iceland, where he was retaught survival skills. Keiko survived in the wild for several years but died in a Norwegian bay in 2003.

According to the HSUS, an approximate 10 percent of the 2,000 animal exhibitions licensed by the United States Department of Agriculture (USDA) are accredited by the Association of Zoos and Aquariums (AZA). Often, smaller "roadside zoos" lack the resources and professional training to provide adequately for the animals in their care. Roadside zoos are regulated by the AWA, but enforcement is a problem because there are too few inspectors for the number of captive animals.

The Debate over Elephants in Captivity

Their enormous size makes elephants a challenge to keep in captivity. They eat a lot, drink a lot, and require more space than other animals. Research has shown that elephants are extremely social and suffer psychologically when their herds are disrupted. This information has led some zoos to the conclusion that elephants and zoos are not a good combination.

Animal rights advocates are pressuring all zoos to stop keeping elephants in captivity, arguing that zoos cannot meet the physical, social, and psychological needs of the world's largest land mammal. IDA compiles an annual list of the "Ten Worst Zoos for Elephants." It cites zoos that keep a single elephant in captivity without companionship and those where elephants are controlled with a painful bullhook.

It is not only zoos that receive negative attention from keeping elephants. Circuses have been the target of PETA picketers for years. The animal rights group criticizes the practice of using performing elephants in circuses, saying the elephants are prodded, whipped, and beaten to make them perform.

PERFORMING ANIMALS

Animal rights activists are also concerned about the welfare of animals used in circuses and shows. While most modern trainers use positive reinforcement to reward animals for performing tricks, there are also reports of punishment used in training. Animal activists say that animals such as elephants, tigers, orcas, and bears should not be made to perform stunts for human amusement. Not only is it harmful to the animals, but it also puts humans at risk for injury when an animal rebels against punishment or confinement.

Too Wild to Tame?

Performers Siegfried and Roy staged one of the most popular shows in Las Vegas for many years. In 2003, Roy Horn was critically mauled by one of the show's performing white tigers. Animal rights advocates say the incident provides evidence that wild animals should not be used in entertainment.

The same problem exists in rodeos. Many competitors are injured in these competitions, along with bulls, horses, and other animals used in rodeos. Competitors routinely inflict pain on animals by using spurs, electric prods, and flank straps to make the animals perform. While ambulances are on hand to care for injured humans, there is not always a veterinarian on hand for injured animals, which sometimes are sent straight to the slaughterhouse after the event.

Racing

Horse and dog racing have long been popular spectator sports in the United States. Thoroughbred horses are bred for speed, as are greyhound dogs. Because the animals are pushed to their limits at risk of injury or death, animal rights advocates are concerned about the abuse of animals in racing. Those in the horse racing industry counter that equine veterinary science has benefited greatly because of horse racing. Since thoroughbreds are valuable, veterinary innovations have been made on their behalf that benefit all horses.

Barbaro

The racehorse Barbaro won the prestigious Kentucky Derby in 2006. But his racing career ended prematurely during the Preakness Stakes two weeks later, when he fractured his ankle in several places. Such injuries are common and often fatal in thoroughbreds, which are selectively bred for speed. Barbaro underwent six surgeries to repair the damage but never fully recovered. He was euthanized eight months later.

Commercial dog racing is inherently cruel, critics say. They believe it is cruel for the greyhound dogs forced to race and also for the animals sometimes used as lures for the dogs to chase. The sport has been outlawed in 34 states, but 38 dog tracks still operate in 13 states. Greyhounds are kept in small cages most of the time and usually have short careers of a year or two. They are sometimes given illegal drugs to make them run faster. Thousands

Greyhounds race at the Dubuque Greyhound Park and Casino.

are sent to research labs to be used in experiments after their racing careers are over.

Animal Fighting

Cockfighting and dogfighting have been popular forms of entertainment in the United States and around the world for centuries. Bullfighting was introduced to Mexico by Spanish colonists and is popular there, but it is not done in the United States.

Gambling is a key part of cockfighting and dogfighting. The "cocks" are male birds specially bred for fighting. They are placed in a ring where they cannot escape. The fight usually continues until one of the competitors is dead. The birds are fitted with razor blades on their legs to inflict maximum injury to their opponent. Cockfighting is illegal in 49 states, all except Louisiana.

American pit bull terriers are the most common breed used in dogfights. They are bred for their strong jaws, tenacity, and aggression. The dogs are placed in an arena or "pit" where they attack each other until one of them cannot continue fighting. Both dogs usually suffer severe injuries such as blood loss, broken bones, and damaged eyes. The winner usually survives, while the loser often does not. Although dogfighting is illegal in every state, it still occurs. To help put an end to the spectacle, laws have been passed to punish not only those who stage a dogfight, but also those who come to watch and bet on one. ⌐

Two roosters during a cockfight in Manila, Philippines

Chickens at the Ooh-Mah-Nee farm animal sanctuary

ANIMAL RIGHTS TODAY

ost people agree that humans should treat animals well. But what does that mean exactly? The answer depends on who is asked and which animal is being discussed. A chicken rancher might say it means providing chickens raised for their meat with basic supplies such as food, water, and shelter. A teenager with a pet might say it means giving the animal a card or gift on its birthday.

When Henry Salt wrote his book, *Animal Rights*, in 1892, there were no greeting cards for pets and few people were concerned about what happened to animals on farms or anywhere else. In time, humane organizations formed to help educate the public about animal cruelty.

PAST SUCCESS

The animal rights movement has achieved many of its goals in a short time. Chimpanzees have been retired from research laboratories and moved to sanctuaries. The number of "no-kill" animal shelters has increased. Fewer scientists-in-training dissect live animals. There has been a moratorium on whaling for more than two decades. Nearly all of the tuna sold in the United States and 50 other countries is now "dolphin safe," or caught without harming dolphins.

Genetic Engineering and Cloning

Animal rights advocates are concerned about scientific research in the area of genetic engineering and cloning. They say that cloned animals created thus far have often been unhealthy. Genetic engineering has been promoted as a way to create animals that would be more productive. Genetically engineered cows may produce more milk, for example. The animal rights community is opposed to creating animals solely for the purpose of providing a resource to humans.

Support for Change

Americans have supported the campaigns that have brought about these and other changes. The question now is not whether people are willing to support changing the way society has traditionally treated animals, but to what degree. It is not likely that Americans will give up eating meat out of sympathy for animals, but more students are demanding vegetarian options at their school lunch counters. When the plight of geese used to make foie gras and calves used to produce veal was brought to light, many people responded with moral outrage, changed their habits, and voted for laws against these practices.

The Circle of Ethics

"In an earlier stage of our development most human groups held to a tribal ethic. Members of the tribe were protected, but people of other tribes could be robbed or killed as one pleased. Gradually the circle of protection expanded, but as recently as 150 years ago we did not include blacks. So African human beings could be captured, shipped to America and sold. In Australia white settlers regarded Aborigines as a pest and hunted them down, much as kangaroos are hunted down today. Just as we have progressed beyond the blatantly racist ethic of the era of slavery and colonialism, so we must now progress beyond the speciesist ethic of the era of factory farming, of the use of animals as mere research tools, of whaling, seal hunting, kangaroo slaughter and the destruction of wilderness. We must take the final step in expanding the circle of ethics."[1]

—Peter Singer

FUTURE ISSUES TO WATCH

Working to ensure the survival of the polar bear is one of the top current issues among animal advocates. There is legislation pending in the U.S. Congress that would discourage trophy hunting of these animals in Canada by banning importation of their heads and hides into the United States. There is also great concern that the polar bear is under threat of extinction from melting ice in its Arctic home due to global warming.

Changing Laws

Animal rights advocates still have many changes they would like to see, such as expanding the Animal Welfare Act (AWA) to include rodents, the vast majority of animals used in research. They would also like to see the inclusion of farm animals, which are the bulk of animals in the United States. They want the more humane CAK slaughter method used and poultry added to the HMSA.

The safety of pet food is another issue that has drawn concern in recent times. In response to a recall of contaminated pet food that resulted in the deaths of many pets, a bill was introduced in Congress in May 2007 to increase inspections of imported foods.

In some cases, businesses are joining the effort to improve animal rights, such as the expanding boycott of Canadian seafood. Their goal is to put pressure on the Canadian government to outlaw the annual slaughter of fur seals. The boycott specifically targets

Canadian fishermen who shoot or club the young seals to death. When it began, PETA was considered to be a fringe group of radicals. It now has 1.6 million members and supporters. PETA President Ingrid Newkirk said,

> *I think when we started, we were about as outside the mainstream as a person or group could get. ... I think that the mainstream has incorporated animal rights' concerns.*[2]

The debate continues as to what kinds of rights animals should have. The animal rights movement is constantly changing with public opinion. What Americans thought was acceptable 50 or even ten years ago is not necessarily acceptable today. It is clear today that more people are thinking about how their actions affect the lives of animals.

*A potbellied pig living at Animal Place,
a 60-acre (24-ha) animal sanctuary in California*

TIMELINE

1866	1873	1877
American Society for the Prevention of Cruelty to Animals (ASPCA) is established in New York.	The Twenty-Eight Hour Law is passed to regulate the transport of animals.	The American Humane Association (AHA) is founded.

1958	1964	1966
Congress passes the Humane Slaughter Act later amended and called the Humane Methods of Slaughter Act (HMSA).	The term "factory farming" is first used by British writer Ruth Harrison in her book *Animal Machines.*	The Laboratory Animal Welfare Act (AWA) passes in August by Congress.

1883	1892	1946
The American Anti-Vivisection Society (AAVS) is founded.	British author Henry Salt's book, *Animal Rights*, is published.	Fifteen nations join together to form the International Whaling Commission (IWC).

1967	1970	1973
Writer Cleveland Amory establishes the Fund for Animals.	British psychologist Richard Ryder coins the term "speciesism."	Congress passes the Endangered Species Act (ESA).

TIMELINE

1975	1976	1977
The CITES Treaty, aimed at preventing international trade in endangered species, goes into effect.	Henry Spira organizes a campaign targeting animal rights abuse in the laboratory of the American Museum of Natural History in Manhattan.	Chimpanzees are placed on the CITES Endangered Species list.

1983	1986	1990
In Defense of Animals is established.	IWC members declare a moratorium on commercial whaling.	The Pet Protection Act, an amendment of the AWA, is passed by Congress.

1979

The Animal Legal Defense Fund is established.

1980

PETA is founded by Ingrid Newkirk and Alex Pacheco.

1980

PETA cofounder Alex Pacheco documents the cruel treatment of monkeys in a neurological research laboratory.

2000

The Chimpanzee Health Improvement and Maintenance Protection Act (CHIMP Act) is passed in December.

2004

California voters approve a ban on foie gras in November. Arizona voters approve a ban on the crates used for veal calves.

2006

The Animal Enterprise Terrorism Act becomes law in November in the United States.

ESSENTIAL FACTS

AT ISSUE

Opposed

❖ Humans were given dominion over animals by God.

❖ Animals have been raised for food and clothing for centuries.

❖ Meat is a crucial part of the human diet.

❖ Animal farming is a key component in the world economy.

❖ Finding cures and treatments for disease would not be possible without using animals in medical experiments.

In Favor

❖ Animals are living, feeling beings and should never be made to suffer or be denied freedom for human benefit.

❖ Animals are the subject-of-a-life and therefore have value.

❖ More intelligent animals that demonstrate a capacity for language and complex problem solving deserve special rights.

❖ Animals cannot give their consent to be used in experiments, so it is unethical to do so. Many alternatives are available to using animals in research.

❖ People do not need to eat meat or use any animal products to be healthy.

CRITICAL DATES

1866
American Society for the Prevention of Cruelty to Animals (ASPCA) was established in New York.

1873
The Twenty-Eight Hour Law was passed.

1958
Congress passed the Humane Slaughter Act later called the Humane Methods of Slaughter Act (HMSA).

1966
The Animal Welfare Act (AWA) passed. It requires humane treatment of some animals bred for commercial sale, used in research, transported commercially, or exhibited to the public.

1973
The Endangered Species Act (ESA) passed.

1975
The United Nations Convention on International Trade in Endangered Species of Wild Fauna and Flora (CITES) goes into effect. It aims to prevent international trade from endangering a species.

1980
People for the Ethical Treatment of Animals (PETA) was founded.

2006
The Animal Enterprise Terrorism Act went into effect and increases federal penalties on people convicted of interfering with, threatening, or harming people or businesses involved with animals.

QUOTES

"If we must kill, whether it be man or animal, let us kill and have done with it; if we must inflict pain, let us do what is inevitable. ... But (here is the cardinal point) let us first be assured that it is necessary." —*Henry Salt, author of* Animal Rights

"Nearly every major medical advance of the twentieth century has depended largely on research with animals." —*The Foundation for Biomedical Research*

ADDITIONAL RESOURCES

SELECT BIBLIOGRAPHY

Francione, Gary. *An Introduction to Animal Rights*. Philadelphia, PA: Temple University Press, 2000.

Singer, Peter. *Animal Liberation*. 2nd ed. New York: Random House, 1990.

Wise, Steven. *Drawing the Line*. Cambridge, MA: Perseus Books, 2002.

FURTHER READING

Bekoff, Marc. *Strolling with Our Kin: Speaking for and Respecting Voiceless Animals*. Jenkintown, PA: American Anti-Vivisection Society, 2000.

Bender, David, Andrew Harnack, and Bruno Leone, eds. *Animal Rights: Opposing Viewpoints*. San Diego, CA: Greenhaven Press, 1996.

Rochford, Deirdre. *Rights for Animals?* New York: Franklin Watts, 1997.

WEB LINKS

To learn more about animal rights, visit ABDO Publishing Company on the World Wide Web at **www.abdopublishing.com**. Web sites about animal rights are featured on our Book Links page. These links are routinely monitored and updated to provide the most current information available.

For More Information

For more information on this subject, contact or visit the following organizations.

Farm Sanctuary
PO Box 150 Watkins Glen, NY 14891
607-583-2225
www.farmsanctuary.org
This organization rescues farm animals, provides education about industrialized farming, and advocates for laws against animal suffering. Visitors are allowed to tour their farm animal sanctuary.

National Animal Interest Alliance
PO Box 66579 Portland, OR 97290
503-761-1139
http://www.naiaonline.org
This educational organization promotes responsible ownership and use of animals. They have an online library, programs, brochures, and educational materials that outline their views on animal rights.

People for the Ethical Treatment of Animals (PETA)
501 Front Street, Norfolk, VA 23510
757-622-PETA (7382)
The largest animal rights organization in the world, PETA has more than 1.8 million members worldwide. The organization focuses on helping animals on factory farms, in the entertainment industry, in labs, and in the clothing trade.

U.S. Sportsmen's Alliance
801 Kingsmill Parkway, Columbus, OH 43229
614-888-4868
www.ussportsmen.org
This organization works to protect the rights of sportsmen and preserve the traditions of hunting, trapping, and fishing within the United States.

GLOSSARY

advocate
Someone who supports or speaks in favor of something.

battery cages
Small cages made of wire used to house laying hens in modern industrialized egg production.

biomedical
Using the principles of biology and other basic sciences to solve problems in medicine.

dissection
The cutting and separating of the parts of an animal or plant specimen for scientific study.

dominion
Ruling power, authority, or control.

euthanize
To put a living being to death humanely.

exploitation
Unfair treatment or use of someone or something, usually for personal gain.

extinct
Having died out or ceased to exist.

humane
Having or showing compassion.

inbreeding
The mating of closely related individuals of a species, especially over many generations.

industrialization
The adoption of industrial methods of production and manufacturing.

moratorium
A formally agreed-upon period during which a specific activity is halted.

neuter
> To sterilize an animal by removing his testicles or her ovaries.

philosophy
> The study of the fundamental nature of knowledge, reality, and what is good, bad, right, and wrong.

primate
> A member of an order of mammals with a large brain and complex hands and feet, including humans, apes, and monkeys.

sanctuary
> A place or area of land where wildlife is protected from predators and being destroyed or hunted by human beings.

slaughter
> To kill an animal for its meat.

spay
> To sterilize a female animal by removing her ovaries.

species
> A group of living organisms consisting of similar individuals capable of exchanging genes or interbreeding.

speciesism
> The assumption of human superiority leading to the exploitation of animals.

vaccine
> A preparation containing weakened or dead microbes of the kind that cause a particular disease; administered to stimulate the immune system to produce antibodies against that disease.

Source Notes

Chapter 1. The Issue of Animal Rights

1. Jeremy Bentham. *An Introduction to the Principles of Morals and Legislation*. Oxford: Clarendon Press, 1907. Library of Economics and Liberty. 6 Apr. 2007 <http://www.econlib.org/library/Bentham/bnthPMLNotes3.html>.

2. "Endangered Species Act of 1973." 28 Dec. 1973. United States Fish and Wildlife Service. 6 Apr. 2007 <http://www.fws.gov/laws/lawsdigest/esact.html>.

Chapter 2. Animals throughout History

1. *The Holy Bible, Revised Standard Version*. London: Oxford University Press, 1971. 2.

2. Ibid. 8.

3. Ibid. 2.

4. Dalai Lama. *Universal Responsibility and the Good Heart*. Dharmsala, India: Library of Tibetan Works and Archives, 1980. 78.

5. Charles R. Darwin. *Notebook B: Transmutation of species (1837–1838)*. 231. 7 Apr. 2007 <http://darwin-online.org.uk/content/frameset?itemID=CUL-DAR121.-&viewtype=side&pageseq=233>.

Chapter 3. A Philosophical Debate

1. Henry Salt. *Animals' Rights: Considered in Relation to Social Progress*. New York: Macmillan, 1894. 9. 7 Apr. 2007 < http://www.animal-rights-library.com/texts-c/salt01.htm>.

2. Peter Singer. *Animal Liberation*. 2 ed. New York: Random House, 1990. 8.

3. Ibid. 9.

4. Tom Regan. *The Case for Animal Rights*. Berkeley: University of California Press, 1983. 243.

5. Ibid. 240–1.

6. Richard Ryder. "All Beings that Feel Pain Deserve Human Rights." *The Guardian*. 6 Aug. 2005. Guardian News and Media Limited. 7 Apr. 2007 <http://www.guardian.co.uk/animalrights/story/0,11917,1543799,00.html>.

7. Gary Francione. *An Introduction to Animal Rights*. Philadelphia: Temple University Press, 2000. xxxi.

8. Ibid. 81.

9. Ibid. 151.

10. Mahatma Gandhi. *The Moral Basis of Vegetarianism*. Ahmedabad, India: Navajivan Publishing House, 1959. n.p.

11. Steven Wise. *Drawing the Line*. Cambridge, MA: Perseus Books, 2002. 36.

Chapter 4. The Animal Rights Movement

1. "Statement of Principles and Beliefs." The Humane Society of the United States. 6 Apr. 2007 <http://www.hsus.org/about_us/statements/principles_and_beliefs.html>.

2. "History of the Fund for Animals." The Fund For Animals. 27 Apr. 2007 <http://fundforanimals.org/about/history.html>.

3. "IDA Mission Statement." In Defense of Animals. 27 Apr. 2007 <http://www.idausa.org/about.html>.

4. "Facts: Procter and Gamble." In Defense of Animals. 27 Apr. 2007 <http://www.idausa.org/facts/pg.html>.

5. "More About NAIA." The National Animal Interest Alliance. 11 Sept. 2007 < http://www.naiaonline.org/about/More_about_NAIA.htm>.

6. "Overview." Americans for Medical Progress. 11 Sept. 2007 <http://www.amprogress.org/site/c.jrLUK0PDLoF/b.933817/k.D675/OVERVIEW.htm>.

Chapter 5. Animals as Food and Clothing

1. "A Tribute to Ruth Harrison." *Animal Welfare Institute Quarterly*. Fall 2000. v49, Number 4. 27 Apr. 2007 <http://www.awionline.org/pubs/Quarterly/fall00/f00harrison.htm>.

2. "Profiling Food Consumption in America." *USDA Agriculture Fact Book 2001-2002*. United States Department of Agriculture. 27 Apr. 2007 <http://www.usda.gov/factbook/chapter2.htm#meat>.

3. "Humane Handling and Slaughter of Livestock." FSIS Directive 6900.2 Revision 1. 25 Nov. 2003. United States Department of Agriculture Food Safety and Inspection Service. 27 Apr. 2007 <http://www.fsis.usda.gov/OPPDE/rdad/FSISDirectives/6900.2Rev1.pdf>.

Source Notes continued

4. "NAIA Policy Statement: Agriculture." The National Animal Interest Alliance. 1 May 2007 <http://www.naiaonline.org/about/policy_agriculture.htm>.

5. Ibid.

6. Albert Einstein. "Letter to Vegetarian Watch-Tower." 27 Dec. 1930. 2 May 2007 <http://www.allaboutanimals.org.uk/ST-Quotes.asp#alberteinstein>.

7. "National Chicken Council Animal Welfare Guidelines and Audit Checklist." National Chicken Council. 5 Apr. 2005. <http://www.nationalchickencouncil.com/files/AnimalWelfare2005.pdf>.

8. "Animal Welfare is a Public Concern." Dr. Temple Grandin's Web page. 27 Apr. 2007 <http://www.grandin.com/welfare/public.welfare.html>.

9. "Factors that Influence Egg Production." American Egg Board. 27 Apr. 2007 <http://www.aeb.org/Industry/Production/ProductionFactors.htm>.

10. "About ACF." The Animal Compassion Foundation. 27 Apr. 2007 <http://www.animalcompassionfoundation.org/about.html>.

11. Ryland Loos. "Hunting Animals Is Morally Acceptable." *Animal Rights: Opposing Viewpoints*. San Diego: Greenhaven Press, 1996. 168.

Chapter 6. Animal Use in Scientific Research
1. "Frequently Asked Questions About Animal Research." Foundation for Biomedical Research. 27 Apr. 2007 <http://www.fbresearch.org/About/FAQ.htm>.

2. "Compassionate Quotes." All About Animals Web site. 1 May 2007 < http://www.allaboutanimals.org.uk/ST-Quotes.asp#drchristiaanbarnard>.

3. Jarrod Bailey. "Beyond Animal Research." Sept. 2006. Physician's Committee for Responsible Medicine. 27 Apr. 2007 <http://www.pcrm.org/resch/anexp/beyond/primates0609.html>.

4. "Vivisection." Twain Quotes Web site. 27 Aug. 2007 <http://www.twainquotes.com/vivisection.html>.

Chapter 7. Animals as Pets
None

Chapter 8. Animals Used in Education and Entertainment
None

Chapter 9. Animal Rights Today
1. Peter Singer. *In Defense of Animals*. New York: Basil Blackwell, 1985. 1–10.
2. "President of Animal Rights Group Discusses Pressing Issues." *These Days*. KPBS-FM. 18 Apr. 2007 <http://www.kpbs.org/radio/these_days;id=6713>.
3. Henry Salt. *Animals' Rights: Considered in Relation to Social Progress*. New York: Macmillan, 1894. 3. 27 Apr. 2007 <http://www.animal-rights-library.com/texts-c/salt01.htm>.

INDEX

ABOUT THE AUTHOR

Christie Ritter is a journalist who has researched and written stories about government, education, science, nature, health, and business for newspapers, magazines, and Web sites. Her writing awards include First Place recognition in the Environment/ Agriculture, Features, and Science/Health categories from the Society of Professional Journalists. She enjoys adventure travel with her family when she is not writing.

PHOTO CREDITS

Jake Schoellkopf/AP Images, cover, 3; Mary Altaffer/AP Images, 6; Svein Andersen/AP Images, 13, 97 (top); AP Images, 14, 19, 71, 98 (top); Danny Johnston/AP Images, 20; Gorilla Foundation, Ron Cohn/AP Images, 27; Julia Malakie/AP Images, 29; Michael Caulfield/AP Images, 30, 99; Gerald Herbert/AP Images, 39; Ohio Division of Wildlife/AP Images, 43; The Waterloo Courier, Greg Brown/AP Images, 44; The Herald, Justin Best/AP Images, 51; Toby Talbot/AP Images, 57; Manish Swarup/AP Images, 59; Pascal Goetgheluck/Photo Researchers, Inc., 60, 96; Guy Palmiotto/AP Images, 72, 98 (bottom); The State Journal, Suzanne Feliciano/AP Images, 75; Jacqueline Larma/AP Images, 81, 97 (bottom); Photo by Ringling Bros. and Barnum & Baily Circus/AP Images, 82; Telegraph Herald, Mark Hirsch/AP Images, 87; Fernando Sepe Jr./AP Images, 89; Amy Sancetta/AP Images, 90; Nick Lammers, The Oakland Tribune/AP Images, 95